Queen
ELIZABETH II

Vic Parker

Heinemann Library
Chicago, Illinois

www.capstonepub.com
Visit our website to find out more information about Heinemann-Raintree books.

To order:
☎ Phone 888-454-2279
🖥 Visit www.capstonepub.com to browse our catalog and order online.

Edited by Louise Galpine and Laura Knowles
Designed by Philippa Jenkins
Picture research by Hannah Taylor and Tracy Cummins
Originated by Capstone Global Library
Printed and bound in China by South China
   Printing Company

15 14 13 12 11
10 9 8 7 6 5 4 3 2 1

Library of Congress Cataloging-in-Publication Data
Parker, Victoria.
  Queen Elizabeth II / Vic Parker.
    p. cm.
  Includes bibliographical references and index.
  ISBN 978-1-4329-6883-0 (pbk.)
  1. Elizabeth II, Queen of Great Britain, 1926—Juvenile literature. 2. Queens—Great Britain—Biography—Juvenile literature. I. Title.
  DA590.P347 2012
  941.085092—dc23   2011038489
  [B]

Acknowledgments
We would like to thank the following for permission to reproduce photographs: Camera Press p. **24**; Corbis pp. **8** (Bettmann), **10** (Hulton Deutsch Collection), **22** (Reuters); Getty Images pp. **4**, **6** (Popperfoto), **7** (Popperfoto), **9** (Hulton Archive), **11** (Hulton Archive), **12** (Hulton Archive), **13** (Popperfoto), **14** (Popperfoto), **15** (Roger Viollet), **16** (Hulton Archive), **18** (Hulton Archive), **26** (WireImage/ Anwar Hussein Collection); John Frost newspapers p. **17**; JS Library International p. **19**; Press Association Images pp. **20** (Stefan Rousseau), **21** (Stefan Rousseau), **23** (John Stillwell), **25** (David Cheskin), **27** (AP Photo/Martin Meissner).

Cover photograph of Queen Elizabeth II reproduced with permission of Corbis (Rex Features/Tim Rooke).

Every effort has been made to contact copyright holders of any material reproduced in this book. Any omissions will be rectified in subsequent printings if notice is given to the publisher.

Disclaimer
All the Internet addresses (URLs) given in this book were valid at the time of going to press. However, due to the dynamic nature of the Internet, some addresses may have changed, or sites may have changed or ceased to exist since publication. While the author and publisher regret any inconvenience this may cause readers, no responsibility for any such changes can be accepted by either the author or the publisher.

Contents

Who Is Queen Elizabeth II? 4

Early Years 6

Elizabeth at Home 8

Elizabeth Playing 10

Moving 12

World War II 14

A Wedding and a Funeral 16

Elizabeth Is Crowned 18

The Queen's Work 20

Meeting People 22

Bad Times and Good Times 24

The Diamond Jubilee 26

Family Tree 28

Fact File 29

Glossary 30

Find Out More 31

Index 32

Some words are printed in bold, **like this**. You can find out what they mean in the glossary.

Who Is Queen Elizabeth II?

Elizabeth II (you say, "the Second") is queen of the **United Kingdom**. She is also head of a group of countries called the **Commonwealth**. Here she is shown with some Commonwealth leaders.

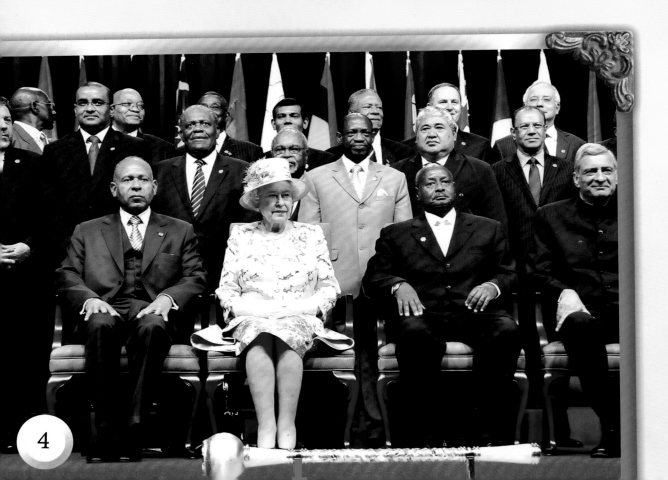

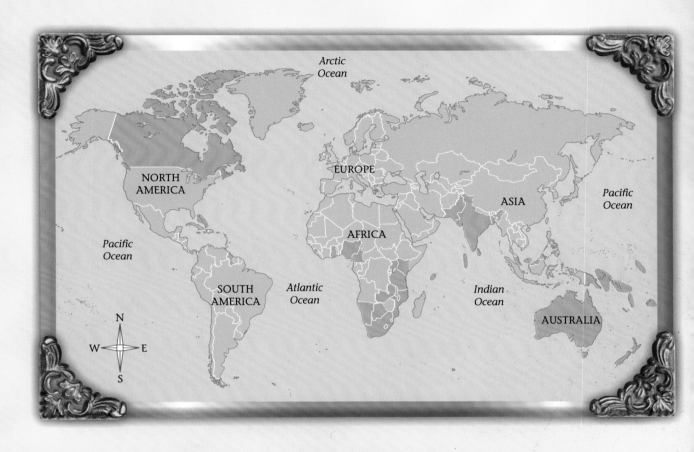

This is a map of the world. The
Commonwealth countries are colored
in pink. The United Kingdom is part of
the Commonwealth. It is yellow on
this map.

Early Years

Elizabeth was born on April 21, 1926. Her grandparents were king and queen of the **United Kingdom**. Her parents, shown here with baby Elizabeth, were a **duke** and **duchess**. Elizabeth was a princess.

When Elizabeth was four years old, her parents had another baby, Margaret. Elizabeth liked taking care of her little sister. They all lived in London, England, near the king's home, Buckingham Palace.

Elizabeth at Home

Elizabeth and Margaret had a **governess** named Miss Crawford. They called her Crawfie. The princesses did not go to school. Crawfie taught them at home. She also played with them and put them to bed.

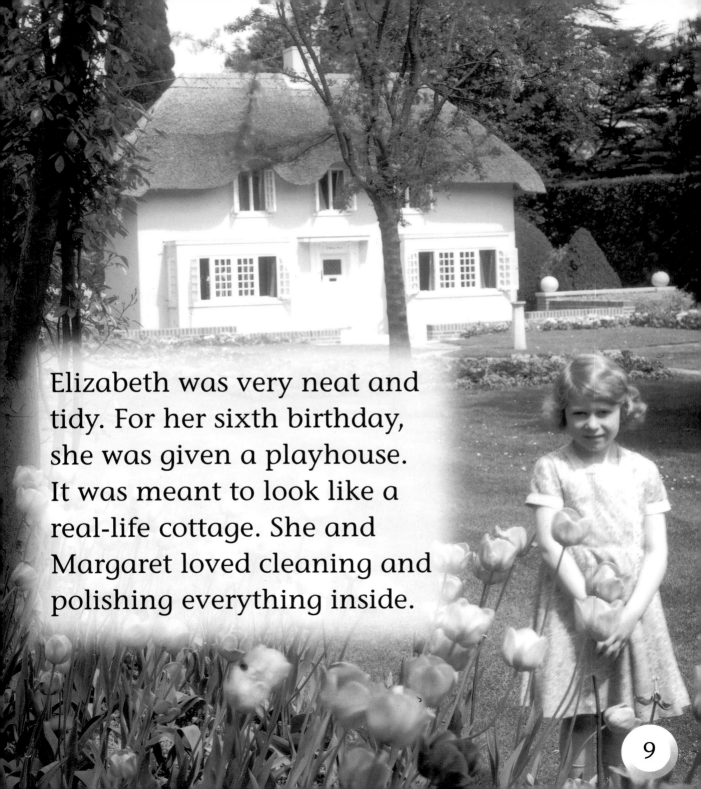

Elizabeth was very neat and tidy. For her sixth birthday, she was given a playhouse. It was meant to look like a real-life cottage. She and Margaret loved cleaning and polishing everything inside.

Elizabeth Playing

Elizabeth always loved horses. She got her first pony when she was just three years old. By the time she was ten, she could ride really well.

Elizabeth enjoyed playing
outdoors. On weekends her family
went walking and biking in the
countryside. They went on vacation
to Scotland, where the princesses
went swimming in the sea.

Moving

When Elizabeth was 10, her father became king. People came to clap and cheer. Elizabeth smiled and waved at the crowds. Later, she wrote a story about the wonderful day.

Elizabeth and her family moved to Buckingham Palace. Elizabeth did not like it because it was big and cold. When she was 11, she joined the Girl Guides, which are like Girl Scouts.

World War II

When Elizabeth was 13, a war broke out. Many people were killed and no one had enough food. Elizabeth wanted to cheer everyone up. She spoke on the radio to children across the world.

The war was called World War II. The British Army needed young people to help with the war work. When Elizabeth was 19, she joined the army. She learned to fix cars and drive trucks.

A Wedding and a Funeral

Elizabeth fell in love with a navy officer named Prince Philip Mountbatten. They got married in 1947. Their son Charles was born a year later. Their daughter, Anne, was born in 1950.

Wednesday, February 5, 1952

THE STAR

No 19,835 ** Three Halfpence

LATE NIGHT

THE KING DIES IN HIS SLEEP

New Queen Flies Home

PRINCESS ELIZABETH, the new Queen, was given the news of her father's death at the Royal lodge at Nyeri, near Nairobi, today. She heard it quietly. Then she broke down and wept.

THE STORY OF KING GEORGE

Colin Frame tells the full story of the Life of King George—Pages 5, 6, 7, 8 and 9.

The Last Day at Sandringham. — See Star Man's Diary.

The first news to reach the lodge came from a Nairobi newspaper. It was decided to withhold the news from the Princess until direct confirmation was obtained by radio-telephone from the Royal Family in London.

The radio-telephone call was routed to the Princess through a little Kenya country post office.

It took nearly 30 minutes for

CONTINUED ON PAGE TWO

First picture of the King after his illness at the birthday party for Prince Charles at Buckingham Palace.

WITH most profound grief the nation learned today that His Majesty The King died peacefully in his sleep early this morning at Sandringham.

The announcement was made from Sandringham at 10.45 a.m.

CONTINUED ON BACK PAGE

Elizabeth and Philip were on vacation in Africa when something very sad happened. Elizabeth's father, the king, suddenly died. This meant that Elizabeth was queen. She flew back to England at once.

17

Elizabeth Is Crowned

At her **coronation** in 1953, Elizabeth wore rich robes and sparkling jewels. People all over the world watched on television. This was the first time so many people had seen such an amazing event.

Elizabeth's husband did not change his
title. He stayed a prince. Their son Andrew
was born in 1960, and their son Edward
was born four years after that.

The Queen's Work

The queen works hard. She often talks about **government** with the **UK prime minister**. She also goes to events like the Remembrance Sunday **ceremony**, which is to remember people who died in wars. This picture shows her taking part in the parade called **Trooping the Color**.

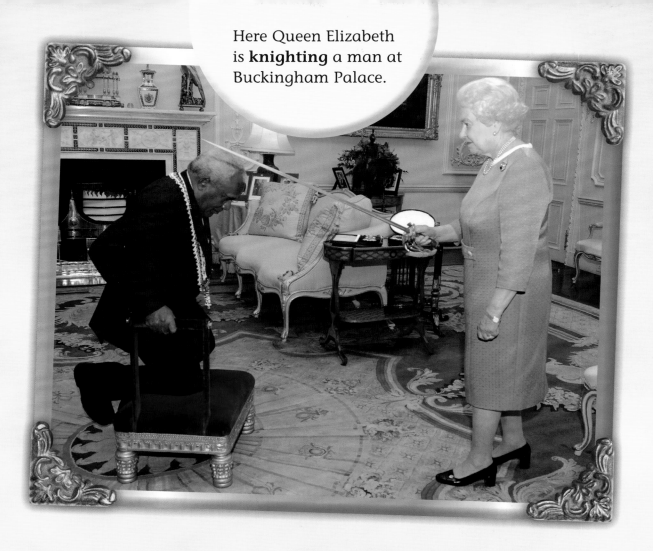

Here Queen Elizabeth is **knighting** a man at Buckingham Palace.

Every year, the queen goes on television to wish everybody a merry Christmas. She sends a birthday card to people who are 100 years old. She also holds ceremonies to **honor** people who have done good work.

Meeting People

The queen often visits towns in the **United Kingdom**. Lots of people wait to see her. She walks around talking to them. Every summer, she holds garden parties for hundreds of her **subjects**.

The queen travels all over the world to meet leaders of other countries. Sometimes she invites them to Buckingham Palace. She thinks it is important for people everywhere to be friends.

Bad Times and Good Times

In 1992, there was a fire at the queen's favorite home, Windsor Castle. Many of the things she loved got burned. Then, in 1997, Princess Diana, the mother of two of the queen's grandsons, Princes William and Harry, was killed in a car accident.

Here, the queen is looking at the damage caused by the fire.

But the year 2002 was a celebration. It was called Elizabeth's Golden **Jubilee**, because she had been queen for 50 years. People were happy for her and held parties all over the **United Kingdom** and **Commonwealth**.

The Diamond Jubilee

The year 2012 is the queen's Diamond **Jubilee**. This means that Elizabeth has been queen for 60 years. Events like this are celebrated all over the world. They are also special for the **royal** family.

Now in her eighties, the queen is still very busy. Recently she has attended the weddings of three of her grandchildren, including that of Prince William and Catherine Middleton. People love to meet the queen and the royal family. They are popular around the world.

Family Tree

King George VI (1895–1952)

Lady Elizabeth Bowes-Lyon (1900–2002)

Philip, Duke of Edinburgh (1921)

Queen Elizabeth II (1926)

Princess Margaret (1930–2002)

Charles, Prince of Wales (1948)

Anne, Princess Royal (1950)

Andrew, Duke of York (1959)

Edward, Earl of Wessex (1964)

Diana, Princess of Wales (1961–1997) Divorced

Captain Mark Phillips (1948) Divorced

Sarah, Duchess of York (1960) Divorced

Sophie, Countess of Wessex (1965)

Camilla Parker Bowles, Duchess of Cornwall (1947)

Vice Admiral Timothy Laurence (1955)

Prince William of Wales, Duke of Cambridge (1982)

Prince Henry of Wales (1984)

Peter Phillips (1977)

Zara Phillips (1981)

Princess Beatrice of York (1988)

Princess Eugenie of York (1990)

Lady Louise Windsor (2003)

James, Viscount Severn (2007)

Catherine Middleton, Duchess of Cambridge (1982)

Autumn Kelly (1978)

Mike Tindall (1978)

Savannah Phillips (2010)

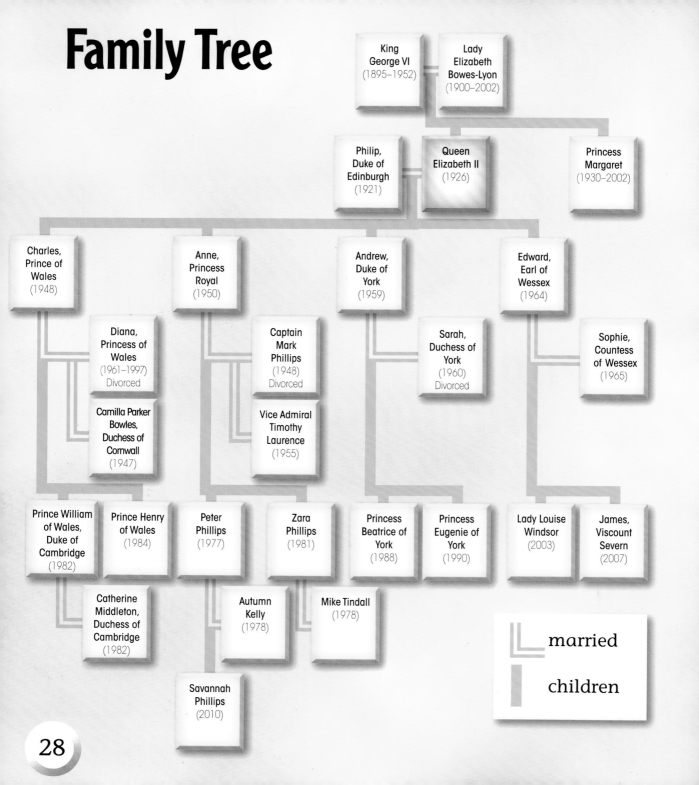

⌐ married

| children

Fact File

The queen's full name is Elizabeth Alexandra Mary Windsor. Her nickname is Lilibet.

The queen's real birthday is on April 21, when she celebrates at home with her family. She has an **official** birthday in June, when public celebrations take place.

The queen owns several homes in the **United Kingdom**. They include Buckingham Palace, Windsor Castle, Sandringham House, and Balmoral Castle.

The queen does not choose the **prime minister** or other people in the UK **government**.

You can see the queen's picture on money and stamps in **Commonwealth** countries all over the world.

The queen receives between 200 and 300 letters every day.

When the queen travels abroad, she takes four and a half tons of luggage. That is even heavier than an elephant!

The queen has owned dogs called corgis since she was 18.

Glossary

ceremony special words and actions used at important events

Commonwealth group made up of countries that were all once ruled by Great Britain

coronation ceremony when a person is made queen or king

duchess/duke member of the royal family, next in importance after princess/prince

governess woman who is paid to care for children in their home and to be their teacher

government making decisions and laws for a country. The group of people who do this is also called the government.

honor let someone use a special title

Jubilee when there is a special "birthday" of something that happened

knighting touching a man's shoulders with a sword to honor him with the title "Sir"

official part of a person's work, and not part of his or her home life

prime minister leader of the UK government

royal anything to do with a queen, king, or his or her family

subject person ruled by a queen or king

title word used before a name, like Mr., Mrs., Queen, Prince, or Duchess

Trooping the Color parade held to celebrate the queen's official birthday. It means "marching with the flag."

United Kingdom (UK) country made up of England, Scotland, Wales, and Northern Ireland

Find Out More

Books

Bingham, Jane. *William and Kate: A Royal Romance*. Chicago: Heinemann Library, 2011.

Ganeri, Anita. *Britain and the British* (Focus on Europe). Mankato, Minn.: Stargazer, 2005.

Mortimer, Gavin, and Tim Hutchinson. *Find Out About the United Kingdom*. Hauppauge, N.Y.: Barron's Educational Series, 2009.

Throp, Claire. *England* (Countries Around the World). Chicago: Heinemann Library, 2012.

Web sites

http://kids.nationalgeographic.com/kids/places/find/united-kingdom/
Learn more facts about the United Kingdom.

www.pbs.org/opb/monarchy/
Learn more about the queen and watch video clips of her.

www.royal.gov.uk
This is the official web site of the queen and the royal family.

Places to visit

If you are ever able to visit the United Kingdom, there are some great places to visit that will teach you more about the queen:

- Buckingham Palace, London, England: You can watch the changing of the guard outside. In the summer, you can buy tickets to go inside.
- The Tower of London: The crown jewels are on display in this big castle on the Thames River.
- Westminster Abbey, London: The queen was crowned and married in this cathedral (big church).

Index

Balmoral Castle 29, 30
birthday 6, 29, 31
British Army 15
Buckingham Palace 7, 13, 23, 29, 30, 31

Catherine Middleton 27
Christmas 21
Commonwealth 4, 5, 25, 29, 30, 31
coronation 18
Crawfie (Miss Crawford) 8
crown jewels 30, 31

Diamond Jubilee 26
dogs 29

education 8

fire 24

garden parties 22
Golden Jubilee 26–27
government 20, 29, 31
grandchildren 27
grandparents 6, 28
grandsons 24

horses 10

king 6, 7, 12, 17

London 7, 29, 30

map 5

parents 6, 28
playhouse 9
prime minister 20, 29
Prince Andrew 19, 28
Prince Charles 16, 19, 28
Prince Edward 19, 28
Prince Harry 24
Prince Philip 16, 17, 19, 28
Prince William 24, 27
Princess Anne 16, 28
Princess Diana 24
Princess Margaret 7, 8, 28

royal family 6, 26, 27, 28

Sandringham House 29, 30
Scotland 11, 29, 30

Tower of London 30
Trooping the Color 20, 31

United Kingdom (UK) 4, 5, 6, 22, 25, 29, 30, 31

vacations 11

weekends 11
Westminster Abbey 30
Windsor Castle 24, 29, 30
World War II 14–15